Anxiety

Harness The Potency Of Dialectical Behavior Therapy To Overcome Anxiety And Embrace A Life Of Serenity

(A Comprehensive Manual For Psychologists On Achieving Mastery In Social Skills And Overcoming Anxiety)

Ernest Strickland

TABLE OF CONTENT

Addressing The Uncertainty And Concern That Constitute The Dual Impact Of Anxiety 1

Integrated Modalities For Addressing Social Anxiety Disorder.. 28

Commencing The Process And Essential Knowledge 48

Understanding Other Negative 60

Effective Physical Activity For Alleviating Social Anxiety 63

Comprehending The Inclination Towards Extroversion Or Introversion In Oneself & Others 74

How To Alleviate Or Mitigate The Symptoms Of Anxiety Disorder 79

Diagnosis Of Anxiety Disorder 85

Act In Practice 89

The Classification Of Stress Into Four Distinct Categories 101

Gaining Insights Into Facial Expressions And Gestures 111

Anxiety As A Comorbid Condition" Or "Anxiety As A Concurrent Disorder............ 119

How To Recognize It? 123

Addressing The Uncertainty And Concern That Constitute The Dual Impact Of Anxiety

While it may appear excessive that we consistently emphasize doubt and apprehension as the primary components of anxiety, it is of utmost importance to highlight their significance. Let us briefly examine these two energies: Doubt pertains to the perception that something may not unfold according to one's desired outcome. There is a concern that you might not obtain your desired outcome or achieve it in the manner you desire. It entails a sense of diminished anticipation. Doubt arises from a lack of strong conviction regarding a favorable outcome. The majority of individuals approach this by targeting easily attainable objectives in regards to relationships, income, personal development, and so forth. When one is governed by uncertainty, one is also governed by the apprehension of potential failure. You are influenced by the belief that you lack the cognitive ability to devise a proficient strategy to address the factors that generate this concern. In addition to this, the concern pertains to an apprehension of an impending event. This implies that the event or situation in question is yet to occur, and if it is yet to occur, it indicates that an individual still possesses an opportunity (albeit limited) to adequately equip themselves for the purpose of enhancing the likelihood of a favorable result or diminishing the unfavorable consequences that they are apprehensive about. As an illustration, in the event that I harbor concerns regarding the discontinuation of my electrical service due to non-payment of the bill, what would this imply? Should I simply remain idle and anticipate its occurrence? Although I am aware of the upcoming deadline for the bill, I have reservations regarding my capacity to generate the necessary funds for its payment. Doubt can be destroyed in this manner. In the aforementioned scenario, I conscientiously take a seat and meticulously document all of the viable alternatives that are at my disposal. I endeavor to explore all possible recourse, if necessary, and I ensure that I contact the electricity provider to engage in a discussion, informing them of a potential delay in payment and requesting them to refrain from disconnecting my power supply. I endeavor to investigate the feasibility of obtaining an extension, contingent upon making a partial payment towards the outstanding bill and acquiring comprehensive knowledge regarding the terms and conditions of the extension. I am currently seeking items within my residence that I can promptly market. I would consider borrowing funds if necessary; I trust you grasp the concept. Concern, however, presents itself as a distinct entity, and it is this combination of both factors that constitutes anxiety. Concern arises from individuals engaging in an apprehensive state regarding a matter over which they typically lack authority or influence. To provide an example, consider the situation wherein one may harbor concerns about developing a debilitating disease despite diligently adopting a regimen of health-conscious practices. So I worry. I am concerned about the impending weather conditions for the following day, as the weather is beyond my control. I am concerned about the well-being of my closest companion and the authenticity of her romantic partner. I regret to reiterate that I lack authority over this matter. Anxiety is devoid of utility, yet its influence on one's emotional state is remarkably potent. The most effective approach to addressing worry involves directing your attention solely towards the aspects under your control. I am unable to exert influence over meteorological conditions, yet I can adopt proactive measures to acquire weather information and make appropriate arrangements. Although it is impossible for me to guarantee absolute immunity from acquiring a terminal illness, I can adopt preventative measures such as engaging in regular exercise, consuming appropriate supplements, consistently visiting medical professionals, maintaining a nutritious diet, and prioritizing my emotional well-being. By doing so, I can significantly reduce the likelihood of developing a life-threatening condition and potentially identify any such illness at an early stage, enabling timely interventions and improved chances of recovery. While I cannot ascertain with absolute certainty the authenticity of my best friend's boyfriend, I can proactively caution my friend and strongly advise her to diligently gather comprehensive information about the individual, enabling her to identify any potential warning signs and reduce the probability of him being insincere. We cannot emphasize it sufficiently. When discussing anxiety, uncertainty and apprehension serve as the essence and core components. Fear constitutes the essence of it.

Attaining Optimal States of Flow

Certain individuals among us are keenly seeking the opportunity for a new beginning. Several individuals devote a significant portion of their existence in pursuit of aspirations defined by external influences, rather than pursuing their own personal desires. Under these circumstances, it may be crucial to undertake adaptations and reaffirm our identity, a task that can be overwhelming. However, it can also serve as a source of liberation as it enables us to discover our true selves.

Discovering your Ikigai is comparable to uncovering your unique state of optimal engagement. Each one of us possesses an inherent flow, or rhythm, which guides our actions and interactions throughout our daily endeavors; nonetheless, a significant number of individuals remain oblivious to its existence. Discovering one's state of optimal engagement serves to discern precisely one's areas of interest, individual worldview, and means of imbuing existence with profound significance.

Envision the flowing descent of water coursing through a precipitous mountain terrain or cascading over a height. The movement of water occurs as a result of its inherent inability to remain stationary unless constrained within a vessel or container. It instinctually navigates its route without encountering any strife. The unceasing current of its motion serves to cleanse and uphold the existence of life.

Discovering your state of rhythm can engender an inner serenity. Instead of dispersing your attention among a multitude of thoughts and contradictory objectives, concentrate solely on the select few that facilitate your state of flow. Lacking adequate concentration and purpose, our thoughts and actions may become clouded and inert.

Enduring the challenges of each day and the responsibilities we undertake can be quite arduous.

Similarly, this principle holds true when we are prepared to embrace our Ikigai. It is imperative that we establish our individual purposes and approach pivotal decisions with deliberation (by embracing Kodawari). The notion of purpose is expansive, however, when implemented in our personal existence, it becomes tailored to align with our unique and specific requirements, principles, and convictions. Hence, it is important to consistently remind yourself to preserve your unique rhythm in order to articulate the significance of Ikigai in your life and to customize the entire encounter.

There exist three fundamental drivers of Ikigai that have the potential to assist individuals in discovering their unique state of optimal engagement. The essential factors driving this phenomenon encompass passion, capacity, and community. In the following three sections, an examination of each driver and a series of practical suggestions on how individuals can incorporate them into their daily lives will be presented.

What Is Passion?

Passion can be defined as a profound yearning for something, accompanied by a resolute determination to actively strive for its attainment. One can consider ardent partners who share a profound attraction, fervent businesspeople who selflessly invest their time and finances into their enterprises, or zealous advocates who devote their lives to championing or opposing specific issues.

Alternative synonyms for passion include adoration, resolve, and fervor. When one harbors affection towards something, they experience a profound sense of gratification derived from it. If you possess unwavering commitment towards achieving a particular objective, you willingly adopt a mindset that embraces making concessions in order to effectively attain your aim. When one possesses unwavering belief or opinion in something, they demonstrate a resolute conviction and are not readily swayed to alter their perspective.

Although passion is grammatically classified as a noun, let us consider it to function as a verb in practical terms. Put simply, the act of wholeheartedly pursuing your passions, displaying utmost fervor, is what sets in motion the execution of your endeavors and designs, generating the impetus necessary for their long-term viability. In the absence of ardor, one may unwittingly traverse the path of monotonous existence, where one is physically present yet mentally and emotionally detached from the mundane patterns of life. While you may have retained a stable occupation, familial connections, and an active social life, your mental and emotional involvement may not be sufficient to fully appreciate the multitude of elements accompanying your existence.

Thus, how does one ascertain their areas of passion? To provide a response to this query, allow us to present a counter-question: To what extent are you prepared to endeavor in order to enhance your proficiency in this pursuit? When embarking upon the pursuit of any goal, be it of a physical, professional, or self-improvement nature, one shall inevitably encounter impediments throughout the journey. Typically, larger objectives inherently entail more intricate challenges. However, if one possesses a fervent passion for a particular endeavor, they exhibit an unwavering determination to persevere through any impediments that may arise in order to achieve their aspirations.

For instance, while both Sheila and Betty possess an interest in culinary activities, it is possible that only one of them harbors a genuine ardor for the art of cooking. What methods can we employ to conduct a comprehensive examination of this? In order to determine their level of commitment towards enhancing their culinary skills, we would need to ascertain the extent of their willingness to improve as cooks. Although Sheila possesses an affinity for culinary endeavors, she engages in this pastime solely when she experiences a favorable inclination to do so. While she may engage with cooking shows on television, she exhibits no inclination towards investing in culinary instruction or acquiring cookbooks for personal enrichment. Contrarily, Betty's unwavering dedication towards her culinary passion manifests in her self-imposed commitment to infuse every meal she prepares with genuine affection, irrespective of her personal emotions or circumstances at any given moment. Merely viewing culinary programs on television does not adequately satiate her burning desire to achieve the status of a skilled chef in the future. Consequently, she diligently accumulates funds to invest in culinary courses, conferences, and the exploration of dining experiences offered by Michelin-starred establishments.

Now envision a scenario in which both Sheila and Betty encountered a hindrance that impeded their passion for culinary endeavors. Suppose their kitchen stoves experienced a malfunction and the sole recourse for rectifying the issue necessitated an investment in a replacement. The approach individuals take in addressing the challenge is contingent upon the extent of their dedication to their passion for culinary pursuits. Given Betty's unwavering dedication to her passion for cooking, it is reasonable to infer that she would promptly delve into her savings and acquire a new stove without hesitation. Despite the potential detrimental impact on her financial situation, she is determined to make this sacrifice in order to persevere in pursuing her fervent aspirations. Sheila potentially possesses sufficient funds to acquire a new kitchen stove as well, however, given her lack of enthusiasm towards cooking, she may find it difficult to rationalize the expenditure in her cognition and thereby delay the acquisition.

Passion is commonly linked to the vocation one engages in. We are frequently advised to pursue vocations that ignite our passion, thereby seeking employment that enriches our existence. However, in the event that circumstances dictate that we must remain in occupations for which we may lack inherent enthusiasm, yet still appreciate for the sense of security they afford us, what is the alternative? At this juncture, it becomes imperative to contemplate the subjective nature of value. For instance, an individual may not possess a fervent interest in their professional responsibilities; however, they exhibit a commendable dedication and effort towards their work due to the numerous prospects that their position may entail. To clarify, their present job may not evoke a strong sense of passion, yet they exhibit a profound enthusiasm towards the potential opportunities and growth it can offer in the long run.

Further instances in which passion is frequently exerted encompass the sphere of personal relationships. Once again, we are informed that genuine and significant relationships can exclusively be forged with individuals who possess similar passions or display passion for similar interests. This concept has the potential to encourage us to prioritize our time and efforts on a select few individuals within our inner circle, inadvertently neglecting others. It is an undeniable fact that achieving mutual agreement with every individual, especially those whose way of life differs from ours, is a rare occurrence. Nevertheless, this does not imply that individuals with contrasting perspectives and lifestyles are incapable of imparting significant worth to one another's existence. Indeed, engaging in collaborative endeavors, be it through teamwork or establishing a business alliance, with individuals who possess contrasting viewpoints can effectively enhance the caliber of creative ideation and decision-making. This can be attributed to the incorporation of multiple perspectives, thereby broadening the spectrum of considerations. Hence, it is not imperative to harbor personal passion for an individual, but rather, to cultivate fervor for mutual collaboration and the potential for reciprocal positive influence. It is not obligatory to possess a profound, platonic affection for another individual in order to experience passion within the relationship and appreciate the value or advantages it offers.

In a similar vein to our previous discussion on the concept of "Imperfect Ikigai," it is worth noting that your passion can also be fallible. There is no requirement for every element of your life to be characterized by an overwhelming blaze of excitement and ambition. Should you be able to discern even the faintest glimmer, be it manifested within a mere fragment of a comprehensive entity, it possesses the capacity to kindle a fervor. Candlelight, on occasion, possesses the capacity to provide us with the illumination necessary for perceiving our needs.

While your enthusiasm for the explicit task or activity at hand may be lacking, your true passion lies in the profound meaning and value that this particular task or activity holds in your life. Political figures such as Nelson Mandela or Mahatma Gandhi did not display an inherent enthusiasm towards enduring the status of political prisoners, enduring cruel treatment from law enforcement, and making numerous sacrifices in their quest for liberation and equity. However, they persisted in the face of adversity due to their unwavering commitment to their causes and the profound significance underpinning their campaigns of resistance.

Transforming Emotion into Intent

Could one not find it truly remarkable to awaken each morning with the knowledge that they are diligently pursuing a purposeful endeavor? Alternatively, do you believe that your everyday responsibilities will effectively contribute to the attainment of your objectives? This is the type of lifestyle that one can experience while embodying their Ikigai. Each day would present opportunities to advance towards the achievement of your life objectives and infuse your daily tasks and activities with your true passions.

The essence of Ikigai lies in transforming your passions into a sense of purpose. Rather than allocating your time and efforts towards conforming to societal norms or seeking external validation, you direct your focus towards prioritizing the endeavors that already hold personal significance to you, thereby making them the focal point of your existence. As a case in point, let us consider Betty, an ardent culinary enthusiast, who could elevate her culinary prowess to the pinnacle of her existence, thereby making it the focal point of her life. Cooking would transcend its status as a casual pastime reserved for weekends or leisurely moments; rather, it would assume the role of her life's purpose, as she seeks to fulfil her mission of selflessly catering to others through culinary artistry. Furthermore, she would explore alternate avenues for ensuring the longevity of her passion, such as embarking upon the establishment of a culinary academy or venturing into the realm of professional catering. Alternatively, she may choose to refine her passion by dedicating herself to meticulously crafting a distinctive and formidable culinary masterpiece exclusively for her own enjoyment on a weekly basis, such as every Sunday evening.

If you seek to transform your passion into a meaningful pursuit, consider implementing the following three suggestions:

Acquaint Yourself with Your True Being

This suggestion may appear to be overly simplistic, yet a significant number of individuals do not give sufficient importance to self-reflection. For instance, one might argue that their self-awareness is comprehensive, yet it is limited to specific facets of their identity rather than encompassing the entirety. You might discover that you are preoccupied with the demands of daily life and have neglected to introspect and identify what truly drives you. The quest to unravel one's true essence and ascertain personal aspirations can be an arduous journey, spanning an entire lifetime, particularly when a significant portion of one's existence has been shaped by conformity to societal and cultural influences.

Once you are prepared to channel your passion towards a meaningful objective, it is imperative to ascertain whether your aspirations derive from sincere convictions and desires, or if they are influenced by external expectations and the desires of others. Presented herein are a handful of pivotal inquiries for introspection, enabling one to explore their inner self and delve into the underlying impetus for their fervor.

Reflect upon a moment in your existence wherein you encountered a pivotal juncture, necessitating the selection between two significant life alternatives that profoundly impacted your professional trajectory, well-being, way of living, or interpersonal connections. Ultimately, which course of action did you choose? May I inquire about the primary factors or individuals that influenced your decision-making process?

What is the singular aspect of life that you harbor a profound disapproval towards? Possible alternative: "It may be attributed to human conduct, societal malady, or a distinct way of life." Could you please elaborate on the aspects of this item that do not meet your preferences? Does it primarily entail the detriment it inflicts upon others or the impact it has on the environment? Alternatively, in what manner does it contradict your moral or ethical convictions?

Subsequently, consider an individual whom you hold in profound admiration. It is possible that this individual could be someone familiar to you or an individual with whom you have yet to cross paths, but who has significantly shaped your perspective or life experiences. What specific attributes or qualities do you hold in high regard when it comes to this individual? Do their mental framework or perspective play a role in this? The principles they uphold or their extraordinary tenacity and diligence?

Embark on a nostalgic journey and contemplate the manner in which you allocated the majority of your time during your childhood. What kind of activities would you spend hours on? What were a few of your recreational pursuits and areas of personal interest? In the context of engaging in role-play with your acquaintances, what specific role or character would you typically assume during these sessions?

If you were to find yourself with a significantly greater amount of free time at your disposal than what is presently available to you, how would you choose to allocate that time? What approach would you take to formulate your ideal daily regimen? Would you dedicate a substantial portion of your time to pursuing a craft? Or would you be engaging in social activities outside of your usual surroundings?

Regard Your Passions with Due Seriousness

In order to transform a passion into your ultimate calling, it is imperative to view it as a significance that surpasses mere longing or fleeting contemplation. What strategies can you employ to effectively pursue your passions? Is it possible to cultivate them as leisure pursuits or recreational activities? A side gig? A new career?

Please bear in mind that your purpose encompasses anything that bestows significance upon your existence. Consequently, it emerges as the focal point of your being. It is not necessary for you to interpret this in a literal manner. For example, an individual who ardently pursues physical fitness does not necessarily have to solely identify themselves based on this fervor. Having a strong dedication to physical fitness does not necessitate achieving the epitome of health and the ultimate manifestation of physical prowess. Nonetheless, an fervor for physical activity ought to inspire decisions regarding one's way of life, perspective, day-to-day habits, and the types of objectives pursued.

To give due importance and devote sincere efforts to your passion, it is imperative to comprehend its profound significance and its interconnectedness with your Ikigai. Consider the tangible and intangible benefits that arise from actualizing your passion. An illustration of this would be the attainment of a robust and wholesome physique as a physical reward for engaging in regular exercise, while an accompanying psychological reward would manifest in the enhancement of self-discipline. Reinforcing your awareness of the tangible and psychological benefits associated with pursuing your passion will aid in your dedication and prevent it from being perceived merely as a skill you possess.

Set Ambitious Goals, Yet Proceed with Incremental Progression.
Pursuing one's passion with the intention of transforming it into a life purpose entails inherent risks and necessitates making various sacrifices. The higher the degree of risk to which you are subjected, or the greater the extent of sacrifices entailed, the lesser the probability that you will allocate

your time and exertion towards the cultivation of your passion. One can mitigate the risks entailed and enhance the probability of commitment by proceeding gradually. Adopting a deliberate pace involves avoiding hasty decision-making or disregarding warning signs. By thoroughly deliberating on how to cultivate your passion, you can effectively address any errors that may occur and regularly evaluate the viability of your strategy. One could also evaluate the impact of their strengths and weaknesses on the cultivation of their passions, and implement slight modifications to their strategic approach.

Employing gradual progress does not entail compromising your expectations. Your adherence to standards is pivotal in maintaining unwavering dedication to your purpose, thus ensuring they should never waver. Nevertheless, by proceeding gradually and steadily, you can deconstruct your objectives into attainable steps or benchmarks and pursue them one at a time. Although the concept of taking baby steps may vary from individual to individual, it is important to refrain from undertaking tasks that exceed your capacity. Be certain to establish tasks or formulate plans that are within your capacity to execute, utilizing the strengths, skills, and resources at your disposal. It is imperative to ascertain means of integrating your passion into your present way of life and effect minor adaptations until your lifestyle aligns with your life's purpose.

Integrated Modalities For Addressing Social Anxiety Disorder

Complementary and alternative treatment is an increasingly popular approach to healthcare, firmly supported by extensive scientific research and empirical evidence. Complementary therapy, as indicated by its name, is employed in conjunction with conventional treatments. One prevalent form of complementary therapy is aromatherapy, which is utilized to alleviate pain and diminish discomfort subsequent to significant surgical procedures.

The utilization of alternative medicine involves replacing traditional forms of treatment with alternative methods, such as the adoption of a specialized diet as a means of addressing cancer, instead of pursuing surgical, chemotherapy, or radiation therapies that conventional medical practitioners typically prescribe.

It is highly probable that regardless of your location, you will have access to a wide range of physicians, including both conventional and alternative practitioners. This resurgence of alternative medicine over the past decade has significantly contributed to its widespread availability. Natural remedies and Eastern modalities like acupuncture have gained substantial popularity in recent times. While alternative medicine is frequently based on traditional herbal and naturopathic treatments, it also exhibits a dynamic nature, adapting to incorporate contemporary scientific discoveries.

Therapeutic Approaches to Social Anxiety Disorders

Currently, the following alternative and complementary therapies are employed to aid in the treatment of social anxiety and depressive disorders:

Relaxation and Stress Techniques

Relaxation strategies can yield temporary, albeit modest, alleviation of anxiety symptoms among individuals confronted with chronic health conditions such as inflammatory bowel disease or heart disease, as well as those undergoing breast biopsies, dental interventions, or other medical procedures. Furthermore, research has indicated that the implementation of relaxation techniques holds significant benefits for adults coping with anxiety, particularly those in the older age group. Research has demonstrated that individuals diagnosed with generalized anxiety disorder may experience greater long-term benefits and efficacy from cognitive behavioral therapy (CBT) as opposed to relaxation techniques. Relaxation techniques may exhibit limited efficacy for individuals experiencing depressive symptoms, though they are considerably less effective and advantageous compared to cognitive-behavioral therapy (CBT) and alternative forms of psychological treatment.

We have previously addressed the topic of hypnotherapy, wherein relaxation techniques are employed to induce a state of hypnosis. Relaxation techniques are widely regarded as a crucial component in the comprehensive treatment of various anxiety disorders, with particular emphasis on social anxiety disorder. One instance of this phenomenon can be observed in individuals who possess a bona fide apprehension towards delivering speeches or presentations in public, a fear that immobilizes them, causing them to falter and experience difficulties. The act of engaging in diaphragmatic breathing and muscular unwinding is comprised of two approaches that can be employed concurrently with the individual visualizing their presence in a prominent assemblage, delivering a speech. There exist four primary methodologies that can be employed in the therapeutic intervention, all of which are applicable for various forms of anxiety disorders.

Diaphragmatic Breathing

Commonly referred to as deep breathing, this practice entails the mastery of diaphragmatic expansion during the inhalation process. If you have previously undertaken vocal training, this is the technique employed to maximize the efficiency of sound projection. Evidently, the objective at hand is not to foster a perception of exceptional proficiency, but rather to assist in facilitating a state of calmness. The technique of diaphragmatic breathing involves the expansion and contraction of the abdomen, rather than the chest. This method is effective due to the fact that individuals experiencing anxiety or panic attacks often engage in rapid and shallow breathing, exacerbating their symptoms of distress. Initially, it is not uncommon to experience a sense of unease when employing this technique, as abdominal breathing tends to draw greater attention compared to chest breathing and may occasionally appear comical. However, by acquiring the skill of practicing deep and controlled breathing in a tranquil environment, you will be equipped to employ this technique during periods of anxiety or stress. Acquiring proficiency in this technique is of considerable significance since deep breathing serves as the fundamental principle underlying all alternative relaxation methodologies.

Methods for Mastering Diaphragmatic Breathing

- Assume a position that suits your comfort level, whether it be standing, sitting, or reclining. Select a posture that optimally facilitates physical relaxation.

Please place your hands, one on your abdomen and the other on your chest.

To optimize your oxygen intake, it is crucial to master the technique of diaphragmatic breathing, commonly known as abdominal or belly breathing. Direct your complete concentration to your breath, ensuring that you perceive a noticeable disparity in the movement of your stomach compared to your chest with each inhalation and exhalation. Similar to the expansion of the chest during normal breathing, diaphragmatic breathing will result in the expansion of the stomach.

- Inhale deeply through your nasal passages and retain the breath for a few seconds.
- Expel the exhalation via your oral cavity. The duration of exhalation should be twice as long as that of inhalation. An alternative technique that you may consider is the 4:7:8 pattern. In this particular pattern, you can adapt the practice of inhaling for a duration of 4 seconds, retaining the breath for 7 seconds, and finally exhaling for a period of 8 seconds.

Please perform this action between 4 to 8 instances, for a maximum of three times within a single day.

In the event that you encounter difficulties in maintaining your concentration on your breathing, consider employing a straightforward mantra or motion that is repetitious in nature as a potential aid. A research team from Italy employed two distinct groups of participants in their study, instructing each group to recite a segment of the rosary or a yoga mantra six times within a minute, aligning with the inherent oscillations of the circulatory system. Both groups found it much easier to synchronize their cardiovascular patterns and increase their intake of oxygen. If one derives pleasure from music, one may also select a song that possesses a precise rhythm and synchronize their inhalation and exhalation to the rhythm of the song. This will promote a state of relaxation as you engage in listening to something you find enjoyable, while concurrently fostering a sense of rhythmic cohesion through the melodic cadence of the song.

Progressive Muscle Relaxation

If you are an individual who engages in strenuous physical exercise, it would be beneficial to consider the following observation: have you ever taken notice of the post-workout sensations experienced immediately after an intense training session? Your muscles have reached a state of fatigue to the extent that your entire body is experiencing a state of profound relaxation, which aligns with the purpose of PMR - progressive muscle relaxation. Interchanging periods of muscle relaxation and tension can facilitate the attainment of comprehensive bodily relaxation.

Edmund Jacobsen, an American physician, originally introduced the technique of progressive muscle relaxation during the 1930s. The method is utilized as a means of alleviating anxiety by cyclically applying and releasing tension throughout the primary musculature of the body. Engaging in this action affords you the ability to direct your attention and alleviate any discomfort arising from excessively contracted musculature.

Individuals who experience social anxiety disorder are prone to experiencing persistent muscular tension. Through the utilization of progressive muscle relaxation, individuals acquire enhanced mastery over their physiological responses to anxiety. It is typically employed as an adjunctive modality alongside behavioral therapy techniques such as systematic desensitization. In addition, it is frequently employed in tandem with hypnotherapy to facilitate the induction of hypnosis. Nevertheless, it is capable of being utilized independently. With diligent application of this technique, it is possible to attain a state of profound relaxation, leading to the desirable outcome of falling asleep. In such circumstances, congratulations are in order as you have successfully accomplished the goal.

If an individual is afflicted with any form of medical ailment, it is imperative that they seek consultation with their physician prior to engaging in any relaxation techniques. They possess the most profound understanding of the ones that will prove advantageous and the ones you should refrain from.

Cultivating Self Awareness
Know your buttons
Emotions don't just happen. Feelings such as happiness, joy, sadness, anger, love, or hate are experienced as emotional responses to external stimuli. Develop the ability to identify the stimuli

that elicit strong emotional responses within you, as this can provide you with a more profound understanding of your own emotions.

For example, in the case where one has unresolved feelings of abandonment from their childhood, it is imperative to diligently introspect on their emotions in order to ascertain whether the sentiments experienced are grounded in their present relationship or rather manifestations of unresolved emotional traumas from their past.

Numerous individuals who have experienced unsatisfactory interpersonal connections in the past bear these emotional wounds as they embark on subsequent relationships. It is not uncommon for individuals who have experienced infidelity in the past to encounter difficulties in placing trust in their current significant other. This phenomenon arises as a result of the influence our past experiences exert on our belief systems, ultimately serving as catalysts that compel us to default to familiar behavioral patterns.

In the absence of awareness regarding the underlying factors that stimulate your adverse emotional responses, you will persistently find yourself in a state of heightened distress. Cease attributing undue importance to your emotions and challenge your convictions. What is the root cause of my current emotional state? What is the root cause of my anger? Can my jealousy be considered justifiable? This form of introspection will assist you in delving into the depths of your emotions and comprehending the factors that provoke them.

Engaging in the practice of journaling can be an effective means of fostering self-awareness. Recording your thoughts in written form can serve two significant purposes. Firstly, it facilitates the thorough examination of your emotions. Additionally, it presents an opportunity to create a tangible record, enabling you to observe and comprehend your emotional responses in relation to specific events. Maintaining a journal will afford you the opportunity to delve into the depths of your emotions.

Personality assessments can similarly aid in enhancing your comprehension of your inherent inclinations and emotions. Once you have gained insight into the origins of your emotions, you will attain a more enhanced state of emotional equilibrium, resulting in significant advantages for your relationship.

Cut the autopilot

Do you happen to find yourself making a mental note of someone's words but experiencing difficulty in recollecting them after a short span of five minutes? Life is frequently characterized by a demanding pace, wherein we find ourselves ensnared in the relentless pursuit of managing numerous responsibilities simultaneously. Once one is functioning on autopilot, one tends to be inattentive and rarely fully engaged in the present.

You might find yourself engrossed with your phone, attending to the children, or focused on work. When such a occurrence takes place, a significant portion of your relationship tends to unfold inadvertently, as you remain less attentive. Subsequently, at a certain juncture, you abruptly regain consciousness, perplexed by the perplexing deterioration of circumstances. One can inadvertently overlook potential issues if preoccupied, only realizing them when it is already too late.

Prioritizing your relationship and dedicating specific moments to spend quality time with your partner will help maintain a strong connection between both individuals. Upon developing a practice of mindfulness, it enables one to fully embody the present moment. By engaging in the practice of mindfulness, you will effectively alleviate concerns pertaining to both the future and the past, enabling you to fully embrace and derive enjoyment from the present moment.

Numerous individuals overlook significant moments within their lives due to their failure to allocate time to appreciate life's simple pleasures. Individuals often find themselves ensnared in excessive concern for the future, causing them to overlook the significance of the present moment. When one is unable to detach oneself from the demands of daily life and allocate sufficient time to nurture and prioritize one's relationship, there is a potential peril of generating a sense of emotional detachment between oneself and the partner.

Power down your mobile device, disengage from your computer, and put an end to the tumultuous thoughts in your mind in order to allocate a significant amount of time facilitating genuine connection with your significant other. In order to foster a healthy relationship, it is essential for both individuals to be mutually engaged and attentively nurture their bond. Allocate a specific duration to spend quality time with your partner in a secluded setting, shielded from interruptions and external individuals. In this manner, you will perpetually maintain a bond with each other irrespective of the circumstances unfolding in your lives.

Seek feedback

Though it may elicit discomfort, obtaining feedback from others has the potential to unveil aspects of oneself that may otherwise remain overlooked. Intimate acquaintances and immediate kinfolk have witnessed us during moments of vulnerability as well as moments of triumph, and they possess an understanding of certain characteristics that contribute to our identity. Obtaining input from individuals who are in close proximity to you will facilitate the development of your self-awareness.

Inquire with your partner as to what he perceives to be your most commendable attributes and what he identifies as the factors that tend to elicit your responses. In addition to gaining a deeper understanding of each other, you will also obtain valuable insights into how your partner perceives you.

Receiving feedback may not always be the most pleasant experience, but at times, it becomes the sole avenue for obtaining an impartial assessment of one's conduct. To facilitate the process, seek advice from individuals whom you have a high level of confidence in and with whom you maintain a substantial rapport. They are inclined to be candid with you, as they too have your best interests at heart.

Ensure your well-being OR Prioritize self-care and personal welfare

By ensuring the well-being of both your mind and body, you equip yourself to effectively manage anxiety and concern. In the ensuing days, our attention will be directed towards activities that you can undertake daily to attend to your well-being.

Day 9: Engage in Self-Care Practices

Irrespective of any concurrent circumstances in your life, it is imperative that you prioritize self-care. Anxiety commonly results in self-neglect, giving rise to additional complications. It is essential to consistently bear in mind that you hold significance. Your welfare is significant and it plays a role in shaping your response to various circumstances.

Allocate a designated period of time for self-care and dedicate it solely to personal rejuvenation and nourishment. Make your nails. Make your hair. Do something you like. Treat yourself to something. Furthermore, it is imperative to establish a robust support network and actively seek out individuals who positively contribute to your personal growth and development. In all your pursuits, give due consideration to your own needs and aspirations, not solely those of others. By adopting a consistent self-care routine, you will reduce your vulnerability to both stress and anxiety. Please bear in mind that anxiety has a tendency to accumulate over time. If you engage in regular stress-reducing practices, it will not be afforded the opportunity to do so. Therefore, you will be liberated from its grasp.

Day 10: Enhance Your Culinary Choices

Do not undervalue the impact of food in terms of inducing feelings of anxiety. The consumption of food significantly influences one's emotional experience. It has the potential to evoke sensations of increased vitality and heightened concentration, or alternatively, induce feelings of fatigue and diminished concentration. An illustration of this can be seen in the way caffeine has a tendency to elevate one's levels of anxiety. Consistent consumption will certainly result in increased feelings of anxiety and stress. This is the rationale behind considering a reduction in your coffee consumption. Rather than excessively consuming coffee, consider increasing your consumption of green tea. This approach will effectively calm your mind and mitigate your levels of anxiety.

It is advisable to also reduce your consumption of carbohydrates and endeavor to consume fewer processed foods. These food categories have been associated with a range of health concerns, such as depression. Eliminating these food items from your diet will result in improved physical well-being and heightened mental acuity. It is imperative to prioritize the consumption of vegetables and whole foods. You desire sustenance that will provide satiety without exacerbating your existing health concerns. Enhancing the quality of your dietary choices will result in increased vitality and improved overall wellness. Additionally, you will experience heightened mental and physical vitality, allowing you to approach matters impartially in a more advantageous mental state.

As you make adjustments to your dietary habits, it is important to also prioritize the increased consumption of water. Water has a positive impact on one's emotional state by facilitating the elimination of toxins and revitalizing the body. So, refrain from leaving it to chance. Instead, ensure that you always have water readily available by carrying a supply with you whenever you depart from your residence.

Commencing The Process And Essential Knowledge

This is a challenging matter, as comprehension often only arises through personal experiential encounters. I was initially truly intimidated by the experience the first time I encountered it. I recollect glancing towards the visage of my spouse. He appeared visibly frightened and bewildered. Anxiety and panic attacks can evoke significant distress and disturbance to one's psychological and physiological well-being. I firmly assert that if you are perusing my book, it is highly probable that you have previously experienced either an episode of anxiety or a panic attack. Am I right? I thought so. It is a challenging existence when one must commence grappling with these predicaments. One may experience symptoms such as increased heart rate, impaired vision, and sensory deficit in various body regions. You essentially experience a certainty of imminent mortality.

I kindly request that you refrain from letting go. Preserve your existence. It will get better. You must exert effort and avoid succumbing to self-pity. Rise and advocate for your own cause. I'm rooting for you. I am exerting utmost effort in assisting you at this moment. So please read on.

I recollect the initial onset of these panic attacks. My spouse would advise me to simply move past it. Indeed, both parties were unaware at the time that the endeavor would not unfold as effortlessly as expected. No way, no how. My acquaintances would frequently contact me, inquiring about my whereabouts and the reasons behind my seclusion. I informed them regarding the current situation. The majority of my acquaintances and relatives were evidently unaware. There may have been a few individuals who had undergone episodes of anxiety. I surmise that their reticence or reluctance stemmed from an absence of disclosure regarding their panic attacks, for reasons that elude me. Perhaps they experienced a sense of embarrassment themselves. Alternatively, they perhaps harbored doubt regarding the accuracy of their diagnosis. Who knows?

This is why I wrote this book, because no one ever wants to just talk about it. I mean, come on. We are all human. Aren't we? It is imperative that we display empathy towards our fellow human beings. I greatly appreciate the instance when an individual discloses their thoughts and utters, and I cite, "Why are you unable to move on?" or "It is an inconsequential matter, cease dwelling on it." This particular sentence resonates positively with me. "Regain your composure." Indeed, that was my preferred choice. I am confident that you have made attempts to discontinue or address the situation, or any combination of the aforementioned options. I would like to inquire: Were you able to accomplish any of the mentioned tasks? Nope me either.

Have you ever engaged in this activity? When one is experiencing a severe panic attack, it is common for the individual to shield their face in order to avoid being seen by others. I frequently engaged in a particular action. I am presently contemplating the matter due to experiencing significant embarrassment, thus necessitating the concealment of my visage. I am feeling ashamed as I am unable to immediately overcome this state. I wish I could. Subsequently, I discovered that traversing the aforementioned task is an exceedingly protracted endeavor. Wouldn't you agree? I have also acquired the knowledge that it is important for me to avoid experiencing embarrassment. I came to the realization that there is absolutely no cause for embarrassment. I mean come on. We did not intentionally desire this outcome for ourselves. We are making every effort to comprehend it independently.

At the onset of my initial experience with panic attacks and severe anxiety. I refrained from attempting to provide an explanation to anyone. I am perplexed by the idea of how I could possibly accomplish that.

Did you try? I don't think so. The rationale behind this is that I possessed very limited knowledge of the situation at hand, making it exceedingly difficult for me to attempt to elucidate it to another individual. I realized that making an effort was imperative, as failure to do so would likely exacerbate the situation between myself and others. I am presently endeavoring to elucidate the matter to my spouse in advance. I am highly confident that he failed to comprehend it entirely. Merely from the expression on his countenance. You are surely familiar with the expression whereby an individual bestows upon you a gaze implying a certain incredulity toward your sanity. Yep, that's the look. When one finds themselves at the cusp of this tumultuous wave of anxiety. Your thoughts appear to be clouded. Your ability to think clearly is severely impaired. Abstain from endeavoring to focus solely on a singular matter. You are simply endeavoring to sustain yourself in this environment. It is indisputable that one must strive to assist individuals who have never experienced anxiety or panic attacks. You desire their comprehension of your situation, thus I shall present an alternative approach that I have personally experimented with.

I am engaged in conversation with my spouse, who possesses a comprehensive understanding of the current situation. I deemed it appropriate to approach him as my initial choice. This is the manner in which I provided an explanation to him.

It resembles the act of inadvertently stepping off a curb without assessing the flow of traffic, akin to the scenario being described. Suddenly, a vehicle approaches in such proximity that it gives the impression of a collision, although no impact actually occurs. It elicited such a strong fright reaction from you, causing you to swiftly step back, and the intensity of the scare caused your heart to thump vigorously within your chest. You were trembling, and your legs displayed instability. You thought you were going to have a heart attack. It may be necessary for you to take a seat in order to attempt to restore a sense of calm. It took you a considerable amount of time to achieve a semblance of composure and improvement.

When I elucidated this scenario to him. The countenance he displayed was invaluable. He expressed to me that, based on his experience with a panic attack, he would refrain completely from advising me to undergo such an ordeal. Once more, I implore you to move beyond this issue. I believe he has ultimately grasped the concept. He has refrained from uttering those words to me since. I am of the opinion that he has become more understanding at present. It took a while, but I think he gets it as much as possible.

It is evident that one must resort to drastic measures in order to convey one's feelings to those held dear. Those who have not experienced a panic attack or do not possess anxiety may struggle to comprehend the subjective experience and sensations associated with such episodes. This actually provides them with a certain level of understanding regarding your current situation.

I am confident in your ability to contemplate alternative experiences that have greatly intimidated either you or others, resulting in a temporary emotional breakdown due to fear. Indeed, fear plays a pivotal role in generating the anxiety and panic attacks that you currently experience. I, too, harbored doubts initially, however, my perspective has shifted and my inquiries into this matter have commenced. I have discovered that this is the primary cause of anxiety, as well as the exceptionally distressing occurrence of panic attacks.

Now we shall endeavor to articulate our feelings of anxiety. After careful consideration, I have pondered extensively and devised the following solution. Presented below are a few illustrations.

This particular case serves as an effective means of elucidating the concept to an individual who may lack firsthand experience. While seated and engrossed in television viewing, an unexpected phenomenon occurs as your eyesight gradually becomes less focused. You are experiencing discomfort in your legs. You begin to experience a sensation of numbness in your extremities, potentially affecting both your hands and feet. This instills fear within you, and you experience a sensation akin to tiny rodents scurrying through your bloodstream. It is possible that you may experience a headache. Now before you really go into a full-blown panic attack. If immediate action is not taken, it is inevitable that the aforementioned event shall occur. You certainly do not wish to encounter another instance while attempting to unwind. Commence the implementation of your deep breathing technique. You may also consider taking a stroll, which is perfectly acceptable.

One could inform their beloved. It is imperative that you make an effort to rise and alleviate your anxiety through physical activity, as failure to do so may result in a severe panic attack, which is highly undesirable. Rest assured, they will either cease their interference or endeavor to assist you. Kindly clarify that you are not in need of their assistance at this particular juncture. I perceive that the rationale behind this behavior emanates from your desire to avoid physical contact, attributable to heightened sensitivity in your nerves. It gives the sensation that they are poised to emerge from within your own flesh. It is necessary for you to engage in physical activity and change your location. Ensure contact is made with a minimum of five items. I have determined that this methodology facilitates the redirection of cognitive processes towards divergent modes of thought. Furthermore, you may choose to indulge in a refreshing sip of chilled water and engage in deep breathing exercises.

Inform them that it is akin to the anticipation experienced before embarking on an activity or undertaking that elicits a degree of unease. Similar situations may include attending a job interview or delivering a public presentation. That unsettling sensation in the depths of your abdomen. It appears that you are experiencing some instability. Inform them that this is the sensation of apprehension. Now there is a possibility that they could achieve that goal.

You could potentially elucidate upon the matter by providing an example such as their visit to the dentist. Apprehension is commonly felt by individuals when it comes to visiting the dentist, with degrees of unease varying among different individuals. They possess the capacity to empathize with this.

I have compiled a series of concepts aimed at establishing a connection between the experience of anxiety and individuals unfamiliar with its nature. I am confident that they will understand it following those scenarios. Despite their potential lack of comprehension. You made an attempt, and it is important that you do not allow their actions to cause you distress. Rather, endeavor to persevere and continue your journey. At some point in the future, they will inevitably encounter feelings of anxiety or suffer from a panic attack, and subsequently gain a deeper understanding of the matter. They may even approach you to inform you that they comprehend the concept.

You and your family members must demonstrate patience during this time. If they genuinely care for you, they will afford you the necessary time to recuperate. If it is at all possible, they may offer their assistance to you during this difficult time. "Allow them to assist you!

Understanding Other Negative Emotional Reactions

Shyness (likewise called diffidence) is the feeling of trepidation, absence of solace, or clumsiness, particularly when an individual is around others. This phenomenon frequently occurs in novel situations or with unfamiliar individuals. Shyness may manifest as a characteristic of individuals with diminished self-assurance. The more rooted manifestations of shyness are frequently referred to as social anxiety or social phobia. The fundamental characteristic of shyness resides in the predominantly self-perception motivated apprehension of how others will perceive one's behavior. These outcomes lead to individuals experiencing intense fear and subsequently avoiding the necessary actions or expressions due to apprehension of receiving unfavorable reactions such as ridicule, embarrassment, scorn, criticism, or invalidation. A reserved individual might opt to avoid social situations altogether.

Social skills development constitutes a pivotal aspect of shyness. Educational institutions and parents may indeed welcome children who are fully capable of effective social cooperation. Regrettably, there is a noticeable lack of emphasis on social skills training when compared to the attention dedicated to reading and writing. As a result, timid students are denied the opportunity to develop their abilities to engage in classroom activities and interact with their peers. Educators have the capacity to demonstrate social aptitude and inquire in a manner that is less direct and intimidating, thereby gently encouraging introverted students to actively participate in class discussions and develop camaraderie with their peers.

The underlying cause of timidity varies. Researchers acknowledge that they have discovered genetic evidence supporting the proposition that shyness is, to some extent, hereditary or inheritable. However, it is worth noting that there is also evidence to suggest that the upbringing and environment in which an individual is raised may bear responsibility for their shyness. This encompasses instances of child abuse, notably psychological maltreatment such as condemnation. Shyness may manifest following the experience of a physical anxiety reaction, and conversely, there are instances where shyness emerges initially, subsequently inducing physiological symptoms of anxiety. Shyness differs from social anxiety, a condition associated with depression that encompasses feelings of fear, apprehension, and excessive concern about being evaluated by others in social situations, resulting in heightened levels of panic.

Shyness can be attributed to genetic predisposition, the upbringing of an individual, and personal encounters. Shyness can also manifest as an inherent aspect of one's personality or emerge during particular stages of child development.

Effective Physical Activity For Alleviating Social Anxiety

Music and Art
Whether one accepts it or not, the realms of art and music present contrasting viewpoints regarding the correlation between social anxiety and social confidence. I acknowledge that although social confidence overcomes social anxiety, your level of social nervousness does not necessitate the need for social certainty. There exist several definitions that can assist you in discerning between the two: -

- Social anxiety is characterized by the unease individuals experience when being evaluated by their peers.
- Social confidence is the attribute that bestows upon us the ability to express our authentic selves during social interactions, fostering an enjoyment of companionship.

In light of the aforementioned statement, it is imperative that we, as a collective, receive affection and recognition from others, based upon our true selves and our accomplishments. However, this drastically translates to excessive consumption for individuals experiencing social anxiety disorder, to the extent that they may come across as antisocial, ultimately leading to adverse consequences in their daily existence.

Social confidence is characterized by a sense of innate stability that enables individuals to conduct themselves naturally and openly regardless of the situation, and is susceptible to cultivation. The lack of social certainty can also be associated with shyness, albeit with a distinction between two categories of individuals: those who possess the necessary social skills but lack the confidence to employ them, and those who lack knowledge of social skills altogether.

There are strategies that can be employed to enhance one's social confidence, such as

• Creating a method that garners and sustains the attention of others.

- Acquiring the confidence to confront challenging situations, such as potential rejection.
- Establishing goals: short-term, medium-term, and long-term.
- Developing conversational skills, such as initiating and sustaining a dialogue.
- Selecting topics on which you possess a solid command.
- Cultivating the ability to engage openly, forming new social connections and professional acquaintances.
- Gradually developing a greater sense of decisiveness, attaining the ability to effectively manage conflicts or confrontations.
- Strategizing responses for different situations. • Developing contingency plans for various scenarios. • Deliberating on courses of action for different eventualities. • Formulating strategies for multiple circumstances.

This might seem excessively formal or overwhelming if you have avoided or feared training situations, but engaging in self-improvement to enhance your social confidence will greatly elevate your character, both in social and professional contexts. You can initiate the enhancement of your confidence promptly by exhibiting self-assurance through assured strides and assertive communication, if desired, you may prefer to initially practice in a private setting. You shall soon witness that those around you will respond to this, thereby instilling within you an increased sense of confidence.

An alternative method to reinforce your fearlessness is to attire yourself in garments that boost your confidence. Engaging in practical tasks to enhance your self-assurance can have remarkable effects on your confidence, such as the meticulous grooming and arrangement of your hair. Should you lack the confidence to approach an individual, it is advisable to simply smile and make eye contact. The overwhelming majority will exhibit receptiveness to this proposal, thereby enhancing your perception as being amenable.

You have the option to become a member of clubs or attend events that pique your interest. In addition to the opportunity to interact with individuals and enhance your social skills, acquiring new knowledge, honing skills, or developing capabilities also contribute to an increase in self-assurance. Take a moment to reflect upon yourself and the situation at hand, as individuals who possess confidence expect others to respond in a positive manner. If, by chance, you choose to express yourself in an alternative manner, such as appearing uneasy or compelled to prove a point, it is highly likely that you will encounter unfavorable responses. By authentically behaving and presenting yourself, people will embrace and appreciate your genuine personality.

If one is aware in advance of the anticipated social situation, adequate preparations can be made. Individuals who possess adequate social skills gather information, acquiring knowledge on a given subject for the purpose of discourse, or by recognizing the expected visitors and venue in order to strategize a blueprint for their activities.

They assess individuals' demeanor and emotions, as well as discern signals that convey interest. There is no necessity for you to reach that particular stage, unless you choose to do so. Merely a few considerations to enhance your confidence and be comfortable with yourself. Skilled conversationalists demonstrate their ability to respond thoughtfully to what is being spoken to them, offering appropriate commentary relevant to the ongoing dialogue. There is no requirement for you to feel intrigued; mere intrigue will suffice. Acknowledge the situation with gratitude.

Self-assured individuals display adaptability in the face of disappointment or rejection, leveraging such feedback to enhance their progress. I understand that commencing may pose challenges; nevertheless, endeavor to overcome any apprehension of failure or rejection, and utilize the experience as an opportunity for growth. The preeminent interpersonal skill is humor, to which individuals of questionable reliability often turn. There is no necessity for one to strive to be a comedian in order to gain affection. Nevertheless, even in the most dire circumstances or moments of despair, endeavoring to observe the more optimistic aspects of life can significantly alleviate stress and enhance one's self-assurance. Every individual appreciates and responds positively to a smile! I hope that this information proves invaluable in assisting you.

Day 11

Exercise:

Consider this situation: The current time is 3:00 AM. Upon awakening, you discover that your residence is engulfed in flames. All individuals, excluding yourself, have vacated the premises. Please be aware that you have a limited window of one minute or less to evacuate yourself before complete destruction ensues. You must act immediately.

Given the limited duration available, what items would you choose to seize and bring along?

Carefully contemplate this scenario, as it transpires among individuals worldwide on a daily basis. Individuals are compelled to evacuate their residences due to occurrences such as conflagrations, deluges, acts of aggression, and other uncontrollable circumstances. In the event of such an occurrence, which tangible possessions would you promptly seize and secure within the limited timeframe available to you? Would you like to retrieve your cellular device, personal photographs, computing device, travel document, specific documents, ongoing project, gaming console, or no item of interest? The items you choose in that particular instant will hold the utmost significance to you. What implications can be drawn from these observations regarding your anxieties, desires, attachments, concerns, needs, and habits?

Should you happen to experience anxiety regarding the potential loss or acquisition of a material possession, it would be advisable to bear in mind that tangible belongings are impermanent entities. Do not ever let anxiety persuade you into valuing material possessions as significant.

Engaging in a period of calm and attentive respiration for a duration of 10 minutes. Recite the affirmation: "I do not define myself by my material belongings." I am devoid of material possessions." "I have liberated myself from materialistic belongings."

(Please consider documenting and sharing your participation in this experience by using the designated hashtag #30DaysBurning)

Day 12

Exercise:

Presently, endeavor to discern the presence of the color blue amidst your surrounding milieu. If feasible, endeavor to dedicate the entirety of your day to observing the presence of the color blue within the various locations you visit. Regardless of whether you are engaged in this activity within the confines of a bedroom, office, classroom, outdoor setting, or during travel, observe the presence of the color blue in the entirety of your surroundings. Should you anticipate the possibility of forgetting to carry out this task during the course of the day, it is advisable to allocate a minimum of 20 concentrated minutes to engage in this exercise at any given moment.

The cultivation of concentrated focus demands dedicated practice, as it eludes us in our swiftly-moving society. Rather than promoting concentration and careful observation, contemporary society instigates a sense of urgency and prioritization of productivity.

The act of engaging in the exploration of a particular hue or form serves to decelerate our rapid and recurring cognitive processes, while concurrently prompting us to recognize the existence of a realm beyond the tumultuous mental states that we commonly and regularly encounter. Through the act of seeking out the hue commonly referred to as blue, one's psyche may liberate itself from the illusory grasp of anxieties, carnal desires, yearnings, melancholy, apprehensions, or any other profoundly affecting emotional entanglements. Do you consciously perceive the resplendent hues of your surroundings when you are besieged by feelings of anxiety? Most likely not.

Anxiety functions to distract your conscience from present reality. Seek out the hue of blue today and embrace the essence of being in the present moment.

Comprehending The Inclination Towards Extroversion Or Introversion In Oneself & Others

It is important to recognize that extroversion and introversion are not regarded as inherent and unchanging qualities of an individual. Both of these two personality traits can coexist with one another. Some individuals exhibit a stronger inclination towards extroversion or introversion, while the majority typically fall somewhere along a spectrum between the two.

There is no superior category among the two, as each personality trait possesses its own distinct advantages and disadvantages that are contingent upon the prevailing circumstances. By acquiring a more comprehensive comprehension of one's personality type, one can effectively leverage their strengths and, above all, proficiently handle interpersonal interactions. Removing the barriers that hinder effective communication and impede the development of a satisfactory social life is a crucial factor. One potential social obstacle is the lack of understanding that may arise between individuals exhibiting introverted and extroverted traits. Effective interpersonal communication and relationship-building among individuals with diverse personality traits are facilitated when they have a nuanced comprehension of each other, thereby minimizing conflicts.

Carefully examine the manner in which extroverts tend to perceive introverts as dull, whereas introverts may view extroverts as boisterous and superficial. These types of perceptions can exert influence on various forms of relationships. Allow me to present the following proposition: individuals possessing extroverted traits may, in circumstances devoid of social interaction, experience feelings of isolation; as a result, they often seek the company of diverse individuals to sustain their enthusiasm. Conversely, introverts may experience fatigue when they are in the presence of others, especially if they have limited familiarity with them.

It is incorrect to assume that introverts are inherently anti-social, as this is not the case. They possess a sociable demeanor akin to that of a conventional extrovert, albeit expressed in a distinct manner. Regarding interpersonal interactions, these individuals commonly engage with individuals in their immediate social circles. The dialogues occur within intimate gathering settings, providing ample occasions for passive observation rather than active engagement.

When engaging in any type of interpersonal connections with introverted individuals, it is imperative for extroverts to place a high level of importance on respecting personal privacy. For example, the unexpected arrival of individuals can be perceived as an intrusion for individuals who are introverted. While extroverts may exhibit great sociability, introverts tend to display territorial behavior and possess a need for personal space, both mentally and physically.

In addition, individuals with introverted tendencies who establish connections with extroverts should recognize the importance of providing external stimulation to extroverted individuals. An unvarying environment can swiftly grow tedious for individuals who are extroverted. This does not necessarily imply that they would experience boredom during an interaction with an introvert; however, when engaging with an extrovert, the presence of diversity and unpredictability is essential.

Despite their contrasting natures, there exists significant potential for an introvert and an extrovert to engage with one another in a harmonious fashion and cultivate a relationship that is mutually satisfying. This is contingent upon the level of mutual respect between the individuals, wherein effective communication can be fostered even in the presence of significant differences.

How To Alleviate Or Mitigate The Symptoms Of Anxiety Disorder

According to Eckhart Tolle in his book The Power of Now, on page 45. It elucidates the notion that the act of identifying with one's mind establishes a non-transparent barrier composed of concepts, labels, images, words, judgments, and definitions, thus impeding genuine interpersonal connections. He diligently delineates how it mediates your connection with your own being, with your fellow individuals, with the natural world, and with the divine. The aforementioned cognitive barrier gives rise to the perception of division, fostering the illusion of distinctness between oneself and an entirely separate entity.

Additionally, he elucidates the significance of acquiring the skill of disassociating ourselves from our thoughts, as the perpetual cogitation of the mind tends to dwell on the past, often fixating on pessimistic notions. This inclination is attributed to the mind's primal purpose of ensuring survival, whereby its sole aim is to preserve itself. The constant preoccupation with the past stems from its ability to provide a distorted self-conception, falsely defining the individual's identity. Simultaneously, the mind perceives the future as a potential source of redemption and contentment, manifesting in various manifestations. Both are illusions. The concept of time is illusory; the sole genuine moment we possess is the present. Consider this, there are no guarantees for tomorrow, and the past, once gone, remains only as a reflection in our memories.

Have you ever observed the workings of the mind? Within our consciousness, there exists an incessant inner dialogue, where the mind perpetually engages in the acts of evaluation, judgement, preference formation, and expressing discontent. One can achieve a state of mental serenity by cultivating mindfulness and embracing the present moment, becoming acutely aware of one's physical sensations in the present, as if roused from a distressing nightmare or granted sight after a prolonged period of blindness. Become aware of the sensations in your body, observe the surroundings with utmost attentiveness. The manner in which you inhale and move reveals something truly extraordinary, for the ability to materialize your existence within this realm is indeed enchanting, provided you remain fully present.

Eckhart Tolle asserted, "By attentively tuning in to our thoughts, we cultivate an awareness that encompasses not only the thoughts themselves, but also our own sense of self." You have the ability to commence the initial action at this very moment. Make a conscious effort to frequently attend to the inner dialogue within your mind. Place specific emphasis on any recurrent cognitive patterns, resembling antiquated phonograph records that may have persisted within your mind over an extended period of time. Allow me to elaborate on the concept of "watching the thinker." By exerting attentiveness, observe this internal voice while maintaining an impartial stance. To clarify, refrain from passing judgment. Refrain from passing judgment or condemnation upon the information you receive, as doing so implies that the same perspective has surreptitiously infiltrated once more. In due course, you will come to acknowledge: there exists a distinct voice, and I, in turn, am attentively observing and heeding it. This sense of self-awareness, this recognition of one's own existence, does not stem from a cognitive process. It originates from a realm beyond the realm of the mind. You, acting in the capacity of the observer of said thought. A novel realm of awareness has arisen. As you attentively perceive the thought, there is an awareness that arises within you - the essence of your being that exists beyond or beneath the thought, so to speak. The notion subsequently diminishes in its influence over you and swiftly diminishes, as you cease to empower your mind by associating with it. This marks the commencement of the decline of cognitive processes characterized by involuntary and uncontrollable patterns of thought.

Eckhart proceeds: Following the subsiding of a thought, one encounters a hiatus in the flow of consciousness—a state referred to as "no-mind." Initially, these intervals will be brief, lasting only a few seconds, but over time, they will gradually extend in duration. In the event of such gaps, one experiences a distinct sensation of serenity and tranquility within oneself. This marks the commencement of your inherent state of innate unity with Existence, typically concealed by the intellect. Through consistent practice, the experience of tranquility and serenity will intensify. Indeed, its depth is boundless. Additionally, there will be a discernible emergence of elation originating from the depths of your being:

Being confined within one's own thoughts is akin to being ensnared in the realm of temporal constraints.

The essential element lies in dispelling the illusion of time and residing in the present moment, disregarding the notion of a previous and forthcoming period, acknowledging them solely as falsehoods.

To be associated solely with one's consciousness is to become confined within the confines of temporality.

Our emotions serve as an external manifestation of the internal state of our mind.

Diagnosis Of Anxiety Disorder

Due to the multifaceted nature of anxiety attacks, the diagnosis of this disorder necessitates a progressive approach. Since anxiety attacks are classified as a mental health issue, the initial step in the diagnostic process involves evaluating the patient for potential mental illnesses.

Mental Illness Diagnosis:
The initial stage of the mental health evaluation will involve a thorough review of the individual's medical history as well as an up-to-date compilation of pertinent medical information in the form of a spreadsheet. Conducting physical examinations can provide valuable insight into potential instances of abuse or self-inflicted harm. In addition, a laboratory examination will be conducted to verify the absence of any underlying physiological condition responsible for the symptoms. Once elucidation has been achieved, you will be called upon to undergo precise

examinations aimed at ascertaining any cognitive impairments. The final outcome of these assessments will ascertain whether you will be referred to a psychologist or a psychiatrist.

The psychologist or psychiatrist additionally evaluates all the medical findings, utilizing their expertise in analyzing this level of intricacy. Additional examinations will be conducted to assist him in identifying the specific mental disorder that you possess. You will then be pointed out to a specialist.

Anxiety Disorder Diagnosis:
When an anxiety disorder has been determined, the physician will continue diagnosis by delving deeper into your psyche through specific questions. This procedure is conducted to ascertain the precise type of Anxiety disorder you possess, which enables the subsequent customization of treatment regimens accordingly.

The ultimate diagnosis is established by taking into account your verbal account of experienced symptoms, along with your physician's observations.

Key Information to Be Aware of:
Upon obtaining an authoritative diagnosis for Anxiety Disorder or any of its various subtypes, there are several crucial aspects that necessitate your awareness and contemplation.

Familiarize yourself with all available treatment options and alternatives.

Although the precise causes of Anxiety Disorders remain uncertain, it is worth investigating the possibility of any pre-existing medical conditions that might have triggered or exacerbated the condition.

Determine whether medication will be necessary, and if so, ascertain the required frequency and duration.

Might the medication elicit any potential adverse effects?

It is imperative to familiarize oneself with the potential side effects, including those that are less commonly observed, and to ascertain strategies for both prevention and management.

Have an understanding of the various therapeutic options and determine the necessary number and frequency of sessions.

What is the expected duration of the therapy and medication regime until the emergence of discernible effects?

Upon completion of the treatment and the subsequent noticeable changes in your well-being, it is important to recognize the possibility of relapse.

Gain an understanding of how your treatment can be enhanced through modifications in lifestyle, nutrition, and any feasible actions you can undertake.

Inquire about participation in clinical trials - you have the potential to earn a substantial amount of money by enrolling in clinical trials, which frequently involve outpatient arrangements.

Act In Practice

The ACT is a therapeutic intervention designed to address a broad spectrum of psychiatric disorders and adversities encountered during the course of life. Research findings indicate that acceptance and commitment therapy potentially offers a lasting remedy for conditions including chronic pain, obsessive-compulsive disorder, depression, stress, and diverse manifestations of anxiety disorders.

The ACT primarily emphasizes our aspirations and desires in life. This entails a cooperative process wherein the therapist and the client mutually participate in establishing objectives for the immediate and distant future, while also synchronizing their actions. - Several commonly employed methodologies and proficiencies while engaging in ACT encompass:

Practices of mindfulness "
The utilization of metaphors and paradoxes
Group activities

Value assessments
Awareness exercises
What sets ACT apart is its effectiveness in employing a variety of methodologies or strategies that address each of the six fundamental tenets of ACT. This chapter delineates a number of valuable techniques.

Engaging in ACT Interventions Practicum

When the application of ACT is implemented, there is not a singular category of ACT intervention that must be utilized. Acceptance and Commitment Therapy encompasses a spectrum of therapeutic interventions that can vary in duration, ranging from brief sessions lasting only a few minutes, to more extensive, multi-session therapies. They generally encompass methodologies that are derived from the six fundamental processes that were previously analyzed.

Interventions aimed at expansion and acceptance, for instance, may encompass a range of activities designed to tackle excessive identification. Likewise, they may involve facilitating the individual's ability to disengage from negative cognitive patterns through practice. The latter may encompass an individual intervention or necessitate consistent practice throughout a prolonged duration.

Furthermore, the integration of self as observer intervention encompasses a range of practices associated with defusion, such as the utilization of techniques like the Observer meditation or engaging in metaphorical exercises that facilitate a change in perspective referred to as 'creative hopelessness.' Equally, a multitude of mindfulness approaches and cognitive defusion interventions are available within Being Present interventions. These methods enable the re-evaluation of negative or distressing emotions, and the options are extensive.

For instance, in cases where a client finds themselves distressed by recollections of past occurrences, it is imperative for them to acknowledge the factual existence of said event, as this course of action has the potential to gradually alleviate the accompanying emotions. Physical disabilities and previous traumatic experiences are among the instances that are immutable and are advisable to be embraced. Irrespective of the type of intervention employed for a specific case, it is crucial that the aim of ACT intervention remains centered on transitioning from engaging with the content to engaging with the context.

Exemplary Framework for Effective Intervention

Wilson et al. have provided an exemplar framework for intervention. (1996):

1. Individuals frequently aspire to eliminate the historical events or the anguish intertwined with them. They have encountered various challenges in relation to 'the problem' persistently over an extended duration. Initially,

consequently, avoidance patterns are subjected to scrutiny.

2. Examine strategies that proved ineffective. The paradox lies in the notion that exerting diligent efforts to address the issue seems to amplify its severity. ACT perceives the logical framework of the problem-solving system as flawed, given its reliance on culturally accepted and language-based principles for addressing problems. These regulations are commonly accepted, as one possible explanation for a psychological issue lies in the presence of adverse internal perceptions (such as feelings, emotions, sensations). Being in good health inherently signifies the nonexistence of such adverse encounters. The ACT educator is endeavoring to challenge these guidelines by demonstrating that actions centered on these principles have the potential to be the genuine origin of complications. The firsthand experience of the client, coupled with their personal insights, is a more authoritative and dependable resource for problem-

solving. The life of the individual is not characterized by hopelessness, but rather by the utilization of experiential avoidance techniques employed by the said individual (Wilson, 1996).

3. Attain authority through the utilization of diverse strategic approaches. Consistently evading unpleasant personal encounters throughout one's lifetime is analogous to persistently fleeing from one's own shadow. The outcome of this situation is that individuals face a lack of control in various aspects of life, as they try to manage their negative thoughts and emotions.

4. Recognizing oneself as an observer or acknowledging one's position within a particular context bears resemblance to the act of externalizing the matter in narrative-oriented methodologies, representing a clear differentiation from the depiction of oneself in terms of content. Clients are strongly encouraged to engage with their mindful self, the aspect that consistently observes and

bears witness, separate from their internal experiences.

5. The inclination towards cognitive resilience or psychological adaptability could potentially be rooted in a dearth of guiding principles or a misalignment between goals and values. Consequently, the subsequent phase in the ACT (Acceptance and Commitment Therapy) continuum entails "selecting a course of action and cultivating a receptive attitude." This involves delineating fundamental values and fostering a determined resolve to reclaim mastery over one's existence, rather than merely coping with mental and emotional states. Voluntariness does not entail subservience or longing. "It entails a conscious and intentional inclination towards embracing, acknowledging, and confronting emotionally challenging states that have been subjected to unfavorable judgments" (Wilson, 1996). Furthermore, there exists a distinction between possessing the willingness to do something and experiencing a genuine sense of willingness. An

illustration could be provided where an individual may exhibit a lack of enthusiasm towards visiting the dentist, however, they may still possess a willingness to proceed with the appointment.

6. The emphasis during the closing phases of therapy is on fostering active engagement. The commitment lies in relinquishing the struggle of negating or confronting one's personal history and emotional conditions, in order to ascertain methods for fortifying one's conduct.

10. Effectively Deal with Your Perfectionistic Tendencies

Numerous individuals afflicted with anxiety disorders often experience this condition due to their relentless pursuit of perfection in various facets of life. It is imperative that you comprehend the fact that perfection is unattainable. Life inherently lacks perfection, therefore, how can one anticipate attaining perfection? We will investigate techniques for managing perfectionism, potentially easing the constant anxiety you experience.

Alleviate your perfectionistic mindset - It may be necessary to cultivate a more pragmatic approach. This will involve the incorporation of different assertions, such as the notion that "imperfection is inherent in all individuals." Perfectionists often exhibit a tendency to be highly self-critical, and one optimal method to combat this inclination involves substituting self-deprecative thoughts with statements that are grounded in realism and offer constructive assistance.

Furthermore, it is imperative that you embrace alternative viewpoints and consider the perspectives of others. Individuals with a proclivity for perfectionism often neglect to consider alternative perspectives on a given situation. Gaining the ability to perceive situations from alternative perspectives can facilitate the transformation of these counterproductive beliefs.

Furthermore, it is imperative that you initiate the process of making concessions. This necessitates reducing or adopting a more adaptable approach towards your exceedingly lofty criteria. You may endeavor to establish a set of more moderate and rational benchmarks that remain stringent, yet attainable. One can approach this task incrementally, as initially reducing one's expectations can elicit considerable anxiety. Henceforth, while strategizing for a situation, exert your utmost efforts and regardless of the result, endeavor to cultivate an attitude of appreciation. Instead of succumbing to anxiety over the potential outcome not aligning with your desires, endeavor to give your best effort and derive pleasure from the ensuing results, rather than dwelling on concerns about circumstances beyond your control.

Alter your perfectionistic tendencies – Perfectionism prompts you to exhibit an aversion to making errors or exhibiting any indications of flaw. This elucidates the reason behind the apprehension of individuals with perfectionist inclinations when it comes to committing errors. You perceive a sense of uselessness stemming from your imperfections. Nevertheless, based on the knowledge you have acquired, it becomes evident that the most effective approach for conquering apprehension towards the unfamiliar lies in subjecting oneself to said fear. This is particularly true as consistent exposure to the object of one's fear results in a significant reduction in fear levels. If you possess a fear of making errors, it would be prudent to purposefully expose yourself to circumstances that bring your imperfections to the forefront. Though you may experience initial discomfort, with the passage of time, you will certainly observe a notable enhancement.

Conquer procrastination - Perfectionists frequently navigate their apprehension towards making errors by deferring tasks. Establishing excessively high expectations for oneself can frequently lead to a greater inclination to defer the execution of a task, rather than investing considerable time in its completion. As an illustration, it may come to your attention that your vehicle consistently exhibits disorderliness, despite your meticulous penchant for immaculateness. Or, you might postpone writing a report for work because you fear that you won't be able to complete the assignment "perfectly", or you might be overwhelmed by how much work you have to put into it and don't know where to start. Procrastination is, in fact, a transient remedy that typically exacerbates anxiety in the long run. The persistent state of unease and concern associated with tasks deferred engenders an ongoing cycle of heightened psychological distress.

The Classification Of Stress Into Four Distinct Categories

Everyone talks about stress. Numerous individuals would assert that they are experiencing stress. During examinations and when approaching deadlines, I frequently encounter this statement in an educational setting.

In times of stress, it is likely that we have a tendency to seek resolutions. Frequently, we turn to the internet in search of expedient alleviation. Nevertheless, the task of stress management may prove challenging. It is contrary to the common belief held by the majority of individuals.

The underlying cause is rooted in the existence of various forms of stress. Each classification possesses distinct qualities, indicators, and duration. As a result, alternative approaches to treatment are necessary.

The following are the various forms of stress.

1. Acute stress

Have you ever encountered a situation where you found yourself ill-prepared to undertake the examination or job interview for a prominent corporate entity? It is highly probable that you have encountered a state of acute stress.

Acute stress is a pervasive form of stress that we encounter on a regular basis. It is an immediate outcome stemming from the demands imposed by our everyday existence that we are compelled to fulfill. Acute stress can be invigorating when the perceived threat is minimal. Indeed, a modicum of stress presents a formidable challenge. For example, delivering a presentation in a classroom setting can be a source of stress and complexity, despite having the confidence to successfully manage it.

Excessive levels of acute stress can lead to fatigue. For instance, the concurrent task of studying intensively for exams while simultaneously meeting the deadlines for your projects can prove overwhelming for you to manage. In this particular instance, the elevated level of stress may contribute to the development of a more complex psychological condition.

Nevertheless, in the majority of instances, acute stress can be effectively controlled. The majority of individuals appear to have adapted to this type of stress. We acquire the ability to adapt and proactively anticipate potential circumstances.

An illustrative instance would be when a student acquires the skill of avoiding last-minute studying by engaging in early preparation and timely completion of their assignments. A prospective candidate may engage in prior preparation for the impending interview as a means to cultivate self-assurance.

Both instances demonstrate that acute stress can be effectively controlled. One favorable aspect of acute stress is its transient duration, limiting the period during which we experience its effects. While it possesses a transient nature, it exerts negligible adverse effects on the human physique. Nevertheless, it presents various symptoms.

Initially, an individual enduring stress may encounter profound emotional turmoil. S/he could potentially exhibit signs of anger, irritability, anxiety, and depression.

Additionally, individuals may encounter certain physical discomforts, including but not limited to headaches, pain in the back area, muscular strain, and discomfort in the jaw region.

In addition, individuals may encounter a range of physiological symptoms, including elevated blood pressure, accelerated heart rate, irregular heart rhythms, sensations of palpitations, feelings of lightheadedness, excessive perspiration, difficulty breathing, and discomfort in the chest region.

2. Episodic acute stress

Episodic acute stress is a variant of stress frequently observed in individuals leading a challenging and burdensome lifestyle. This form of stress bears resemblance to the initial category. This occurrence is of greater frequency than the aforementioned alternative.

Individuals afflicted with episodic acute stress often display a persistent inclination towards chronic time pressure, yet consistently fall short in meeting established deadlines. Furthermore, it is characteristic of individuals in question to consistently undertake tasks beyond their capabilities, subsequently discovering their inability to manage said responsibilities.

In the absence of treatment, episodic stress can have a considerable impact on an individual's abilities and overall functioning in their day-to-day life. He or she may encounter challenges in their professional endeavors and personal relationships.

Individuals experiencing episodic acute stress also exhibit physiological symptoms, including migraines, hypertension, headaches, and chest pains.

They exhibit a tendency to display hostility towards others, which can subsequently lead to the deterioration of relationships and the emergence of various misunderstandings.

Similar to the approach taken in addressing other forms of stress, the management of episodic acute stress may require the intervention of qualified healthcare professionals. The treatment duration may extend for several months or more.

Nevertheless, the therapy can pose difficulties. Individuals afflicted by this form of stress exhibit a certain degree of aversion towards embracing or embracing change. They hold the belief that there are no inherent flaws within themselves. Their sole motivation for persevering in the course of treatment lies in their earnest desire to alleviate and address the physical anguish and distress they experience.

3. Chronic stress

Chronic stress is a distinct form of stress that frequently leads to the exhaustion of an individual. Individuals experiencing such stress may perceive themselves as being trapped in an unfavorable circumstance, devoid of any opportunities for escape. This perception gives rise to persistent depressive tendencies.

There are numerous factors contributing to the experience of stress among individuals. The primary factors predominantly consist of health-related concerns, alcohol consumption, unsatisfactory marital circumstances, instances of violence, and various forms of discrimination.

Nevertheless, certain factors contributing to chronic stress are rooted in adverse childhood experiences. Possible maltreatment, instances of child abuse, and other distressing experiences that individuals may currently endure.

Chronic stress can kill. A significant number of individuals afflicted chose to take their own lives. The typical outcomes include instances of self-inflicted mortality, cerebrovascular incidents, cardiac episodes, acts of aggression, and occasional malignancies.

Managing chronic stress can pose significant challenges in terms of finding effective treatments. It necessitates the assistance of individuals with expertise in the field. The conventional approach entails the integration of medical, behavioral, and stress management techniques.

4. Post-traumatic Stress Disorder (PTSD)

Post-traumatic stress disorder (PTSD) arises from the experience of alarming or traumatic events, resulting in an extreme form of stress response. Some of the typical occurrences encompass childhood maltreatment, socioeconomic disadvantage, instances of violence, armed conflicts, and so forth.

Post-traumatic disorder commonly presents itself in individuals who have served as soldiers and have been exposed to the ravages of war or have endured deeply distressing and cataclysmic events. An illustrative example would be the increase in diagnoses of Post-Traumatic Stress Disorder (PTSD) among Americans subsequent to the September 11 attack.

Individuals with post-traumatic stress disorder (PTSD) may encounter recollections of the distressing incident, manifesting as recurring visual images or sensory experiences, leading to difficulties in achieving restful sleep. Moreover, individuals afflicted with post-traumatic stress disorder may experience sensations of remorse, despair, apathy, and apprehension.

Similar to other forms of stress, post-traumatic stress disorder (PTSD) can exert an adverse influence on an individual's day-to-day capabilities and performance. An individual's ability to exert effectiveness within the workplace is compromised as a result of the prevailing symptoms. Indeed, in certain instances, individuals afflicted with post-traumatic stress disorder encounter difficulties pertaining to their intimate relationships and social interactions.

Adverse consequences do not always accompany stress. It has the potential to enhance our effectiveness on certain occasions. Nevertheless, individuals exhibit distinct reactions to events that cause stress. Consequently, the symptoms may vary among individuals.

Maintaining an active lifestyle and cultivating strong social connections are among the most effective strategies to mitigate stress. Numerous studies have elucidated that social interactions have the propensity to induce happiness in individuals.

Nevertheless, should you encounter physical manifestations indicative of stress, such as migraines, muscular tension, sleeplessness, or discomfort in the back region, it is advisable to seek assistance from a qualified expert.

Should one fail to communicate their stress with others, it may manifest as a heavy burden. Individuals who experience inadequate social connectivity encounter difficulties in overcoming depression. Individuals who engage in frequent communication with their close acquaintances tend to experience enhanced emotional and psychological well-being.

Gaining Insights Into Facial Expressions And Gestures

Primarily, individuals tend to direct their attention towards the facial expressions when attempting to comprehend others. They hold the belief that any insight into the thoughts or feelings of the other individual can only be gleaned through observing their facial expressions. To a certain extent, this statement holds true—instinctively, individuals tend to direct their attention towards the face as the initial focal point. When engaging in conversation, it is customary to direct your gaze towards the individual's visage as part of your efforts to discern their thoughts and perspectives. When engaging in this action, you are considering and assessing various elements, demonstrating respect and acknowledgment by direct visual contact. Nevertheless, you will also be examining them from various other perspectives. As you observe their overall countenance, it is worth noting that their eyebrows and mouth can provide further insight into their character and intentions.

In essence, the facial area presents itself as a convenient point of initiation—however, it is also subjected to deliberate manipulation by individuals seeking to conceal their emotions. In the event that one observes someone attempting to deceive, it is highly likely that their true intentions will inadvertently become apparent through their visage—such individuals will ascertain the need to modify their facial expressions in an endeavor to deceive you. While this provides a commendable foundation, it is imperative to bear in mind that it must be considered in conjunction with all other facets encompassing facial characteristics and gestures, a concept that will be elucidated comprehensively within the pages of this book.

In this chapter, we aim to accomplish several important goals: We will discern the common facial expressions that one can anticipate, regardless of the individual's characteristics. Subsequently, we shall proceed methodically, examining each facial feature in order to analyze prevalent forms of nonverbal communication. Specifically, we will be addressing the visual aspect of the eyes, eyebrows, forehead, cheeks, lips, and mouth.

Universal Expressions
Are you aware of the fact that there exist certain universally shared human expressions? A shared characteristic exists among all cultures, and it manifests in the form of seven common elements. They are frequently denoted as ubiquitous expressions, and they bolster the notion that specific emotions are widely pervasive irrespective of cultural differences. These universal expressions are precisely what they may sound like—they will be identified by anyone around the world no matter

where they come from, and they can actually be found in blind individuals that have never actually seen another person's face before.

If this proposition seems implausible, consider canines. By removing a newborn puppy from its mother and nurturing it, there exist specific elements of its nonverbal communication that are universally manifested, irrespective of their understanding of the wag's significance. As humans, similar to canines, we possess a designated repertoire of universally understood nonverbal cues. Undoubtedly, relocating a dog from the United States to Japan would not hinder its ability to engage in communication with fellow canines through the means of non-verbal expressions. Similarly, your gestures and manners will be acknowledged irrespective of your global whereabouts.

Happiness

The experience of joy arises when one has fulfilled their requirements or accomplished an activity that proves gratifying or agreeable. In a broad sense, happiness is typically manifested through body language that conveys a sense of ease and, on occasion, fervor. Alternatively, one might observe the presence of a smile that reveals one's teeth, or the mouth assuming a closed position with the lips curving upwards. Regardless of the chosen course of action, it is essential to diligently observe the Duchenne smile, a genuine expression characterized by the subtle crinkling of the eye corners. This serves as evidence that happiness is genuine and not merely intended to deceive you. Furthermore, it is worth noting that the eyebrows may also be raised.

Sadness

Sadness is arguably the most challenging emotion to counterfeit as it possesses unmistakable attributes. Specifically, it can be anticipated that the eyebrows will undergo a descent while the inner corners elevate and converge. This leads to the appearance of creases both between and above the eyebrows. Moreover, it can be observed that the jaw ascends concomitantly with the protrusion of the lower lip.

Anger

Irritation will engage the entirety of the facial area. When encountering an individual who is experiencing anger, one may observe the simultaneous contraction of their eyebrows, causing them to descend and form a V-shaped furrow. The ocular muscles commonly contract and the gaze appears stern, causing the eyelids to constrict. Moreover, one can anticipate observing the compulsion of the lips to constrict into a slender crease, or alternatively, they may remain ajar in a rectangular configuration. When in a closed position, the jaw may exhibit either tension or protrusion.

Fear

Fear can be discerned through the movement of the eyebrows, as they elevate and converge towards the center of the forehead. This gives rise to a concerning crease, causing the eyebrows to level rather than curve upwards. As this occurrence takes place, you will observe that the upper eyelid ascends to enable the visibility of the areas above the iris, as opposed to below it. Simultaneously, the mouth usually exhibits an open position accompanied by retracted lips.

Surprise

The confusion between surprise and fear can often arise due to the shared visual indication of widened eyes, thus leading to their occasional misinterpretation. Nevertheless, it should be anticipated that in the case of surprise, the white area surrounding the iris will be visible in its entirety, rather than solely above it. Furthermore, it is to be anticipated that one will observe the presence of furrows on the forehead, accompanied by a relaxed and dales jaw exhibiting an absence of strain. The eyebrows will assume an arched and curved shape as they elevate, and typically, the skin in the area between the eyebrow and the eye will be stretched tightly.

Contempt

In instances where one observes contempt in another individual, it is often discernible by the subtle elevation of a single corner of the mouth and eyebrow. It manifests as a fleeting, evanescent sneer, often subsiding within a brief interval of one to two seconds.

Disgust

Disgust serves a crucial purpose in facilitating expression, aiding in its memorization. You can anticipate an inward contraction of the facial muscles, driven by repugnance, serving to safeguard the delicate sensory organs of the eyes, nose, and mouth. Such precautionary measures are necessitated to prevent any harm caused by potential toxins or contaminants. The eyebrows descend to provide a protective cover for the eyes, whilst the lips move upwards and the nose creases in an effort to safeguard the nasal region. Additionally, the cheeks will constrict upwards in order to provide protection to the eyes.

Anxiety As A Comorbid Condition" Or "Anxiety As A Concurrent Disorder

Anxiety is indicative of a broader condition and should not be considered as a standalone disorder. We indeed possess anxiety disorders, and each of them encompasses noticeable levels of anxiety. However, as previously elucidated in preceding chapters, these disorders encompass additional manifestations beyond anxiety, and the characteristics of the anxiety differ contingent upon the specific disorder. Hence, it is unsurprising that anxiety is a characteristic manifestation observed in numerous disorders. Additionally, it is worth noting that anxiety is a typical reaction to a plethora of circumstances in an individual's daily existence, and it is a prevalent response to any situation that engenders significant ambiguity. Whether we deem it necessary to provide treatment for those circumstances hinges upon various factors.

In the following chapter, we shall delve into scenarios where anxiety is evident, yet lacks the defining features of an anxiety disorder. As I have underscored consistently in this literature, anxiety is a typical reaction, and despite our possible aversion to the unease that accompanies anxiety, it should not be considered our adversary. In instances where anxiety is observed, it is advisable to exercise caution in immediately presuming that the objective is to eradicate the anxiety. It would be myopic to do so, as mitigating anxiety could potentially exacerbate our exposure to detrimental outcomes. For instance, it is imperative for first responders to exhibit a sense of heightened vigilance as they frequently encounter circumstances that have the potential to jeopardize lives. They should remain vigilant. Our approach does not focus on completely eradicating their anxiety; rather, it centers on equipping them with the skills to operate at a proficient level despite the presence of anxiety.

Anxiety as a Co-occurring Symptom

Anxiety, as a manifestation, is present in numerous conditions that are not categorized as anxiety disorders. As an illustration, it is uncommon for individuals afflicted with depression to not concurrently manifest symptoms of anxiety. The topic of the influential association between anxiety and depression has been a subject of longstanding and vigorous debate. To our perception, there exists a discernible distinction between anxiety and depression, prompting us to surmise that they must inherently possess dissimilar qualities. Anxiety and depression exhibit overlapping biological and psychological elements.

Anxiety may also manifest in multiple disorders where the core features of anxiety do not coincide with the symptoms of the disorder, as is the case with depression. For instance, any disarray that hinders our capacity to operate effectively usually heightens our feelings of distress due to concerns regarding the possible ramifications on our daily existence. In this scenario, anxiety can be regarded as a responsive manifestation indicating the presence of an underlying issue. Additionally, it serves as a responsive indicator which compels the individual to actively pursue suitable intervention for the issue that engenders the potential for inadequacy. In nearly every scenario where anxiety arises as a response to the disturbances linked with another disorder, it would be preferable to address the underlying factors that induce anxiety, rather than treating the anxiety itself.

How To Recognize It?

When embarking upon a relationship, the onset of the initial stage may induce a sense of apprehension and unease, accompanied by myriad inquiries, each vying for resolution. One starts to ponder: "Does he/she genuinely hold affection for me?" "Will this endeavor prove successful?" "To what extent will this relationship progress in seriousness?"

It is disheartening to acknowledge that these concerns persist even in the subsequent phases of the relationship, where one becomes overwhelmed by anxiety. As the level of closeness and intimacy deepens within a relationship, the magnitude of anxiety exhibited in that relationship tends to increase.

The apprehension, strain, and disquietude pertaining to your interpersonal connections can engender a sense of solitude and despondency. It is possible that you may unintentionally create a sense of detachment between you and your beloved. Another solemn repercussion of anxiety resides in its capacity to cause individuals to relinquish love in its entirety. Such circumstances can be profoundly disheartening, as love possesses an inherent beauty. It is crucial to gain insight into the underlying factors that contribute to one's heightened anxiety within a relationship, as well as the reasons behind one's prevailing feelings of insecurity and excessive attachment.

The experience of falling in love incurs various demands that surpass one's imagination, presenting a multitude of challenges. The greater your attachment to an individual, the higher the potential for loss. How ironic is that? The profound sense of affection and the profound emotions that accompany it consciously and subconsciously engender apprehension concerning potential emotional harm and uncertainty within oneself.

Curiously, this apprehension arises from receiving treatment in your relationship that precisely aligns with your desired treatment. Upon the onset of genuine affection or when subjected to gentle and compassionate treatment, which may appear unfamiliar, feelings of anxiety might arise.

Frequently, the occurrence of anxiety is not solely attributable to the events unfolding within your relationship with your partner. The internal dialogue and cognitive processes that one engages in, concerning these events, are ultimately responsible for the manifestation of anxiety. Your most prominent evaluator, often referred to as the "harsh coach" residing within your consciousness, possesses the ability to critique you and provide detrimental guidance that will ultimately strengthen your apprehension towards developing emotional closeness. This critical individual is the one who proposes the idea to you that:

You lack intellectual prowess; it is only a matter of time before they grow weary of your presence.

You will never encounter an individual who will genuinely love you, thus why make an effort?

Do not place your trust in them; they are likely in pursuit of a superior candidate.

They do not possess genuine affection for you. Please vacate the premises before you sustain any injuries."

This suggests that the internalized influence of a coach-like figure in one's mind seeks to exert control over one's thoughts and emotions, resulting in self-estrangement and a potential breakdown of relationships with loved ones. It fosters animosity, and you eventually realize that you become increasingly suspicious. One starts to harbor doubts regarding every action undertaken by their partner, resulting in a decline in their own self-worth and the emergence of detrimental feelings of suspicion, wariness, possessiveness, unease, and tension.

The coach's actions continuously implant ideas into your mind that endanger your happiness and cause you to fret over your relationship, rather than enabling you to fully embrace and relish it. When one's attention becomes excessively fixated on these detrimental thoughts, it hinders the genuine bond shared in a relationship, which encompasses constructive communication and affection with one's partner.

You promptly realize that you are responding to superfluous matters and articulating discourteous and detrimental comments. Additionally, you may exhibit immature or nurturing behavior towards your partner.

An example of this would be if your significant other returns home from work and expresses a lack of appetite, politely declining the dinner that is being offered. When you are alone and have had some time to ponder, your internal critic launches into a fury of questioning, demanding, "In what way could they possibly reject the culinary offering I have presented?" What has been their dietary intake throughout the day? By whom has sustenance been provided to them in their workplace?

May I truly place my trust in them?" These contemplations have the capacity to persistently burgeon in your psyche, rendering you insecure, incensed, and volatile the following morning. You may adopt a demeanor of detachment or resentment, thereby potentially alienating your partner and exacerbating their feelings of frustration and defensiveness. They will be unaware of the thoughts within your mind, thus perceiving your actions as unexpected or abrupt.

Within a brief span of time, you have adeptly altered the dynamics of your relationship. Rather than relishing the time you are together, you might squander an entire day experiencing distress and a sense of detachment from one another. Your actions have not only initiated but also established the distance that you have long been afraid of. The determining factor behind this sequence of events does not stem directly from the circumstances at hand, but rather from the presence of an influential internal narrative that impaired your judgment, warped your perspective, instilled negative beliefs, and ultimately guided you towards a calamitous trajectory.

www.ingramcontent.com/pod-product-compliance
Lightning Source LLC
Chambersburg PA
CBHW050253120526
44590CB00016B/2328